———————————— as ——— so ————————————
       above
                below

To my grampy, who delighted the ears of this child with tales of Dangerous Dan McGrew!

I Am Also You

Hello

How do you do?
i am also you
know what I say is true
i am because we are!

for your recollection
we're all just reflections
made from dust of a star

so whenever i greet you
it's you who you'll meet, too
Isn't that kinda bizarre?

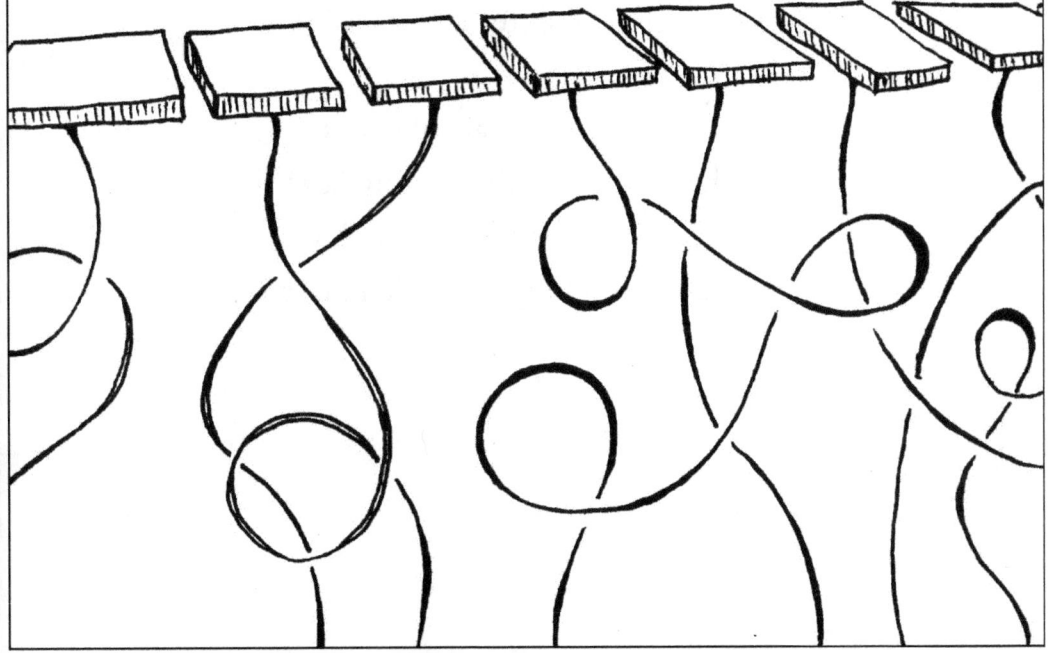

My Myth

Cool black sand between my toes
shifting dunes that ebb and flow
erupting sky with fractured light
consuming wind, at endless height

twisting, flicking up the sand
freezing fingers, searching hands
all across this fluid land

the grandest ship just seized me now
i fly on up to catch it's bow
clutching, grasping, holding tight
my deep laughter fills the night

faster, darker, air fills mast
how long can this feeling last?
forever ever and then a day
before too long i've sailed away

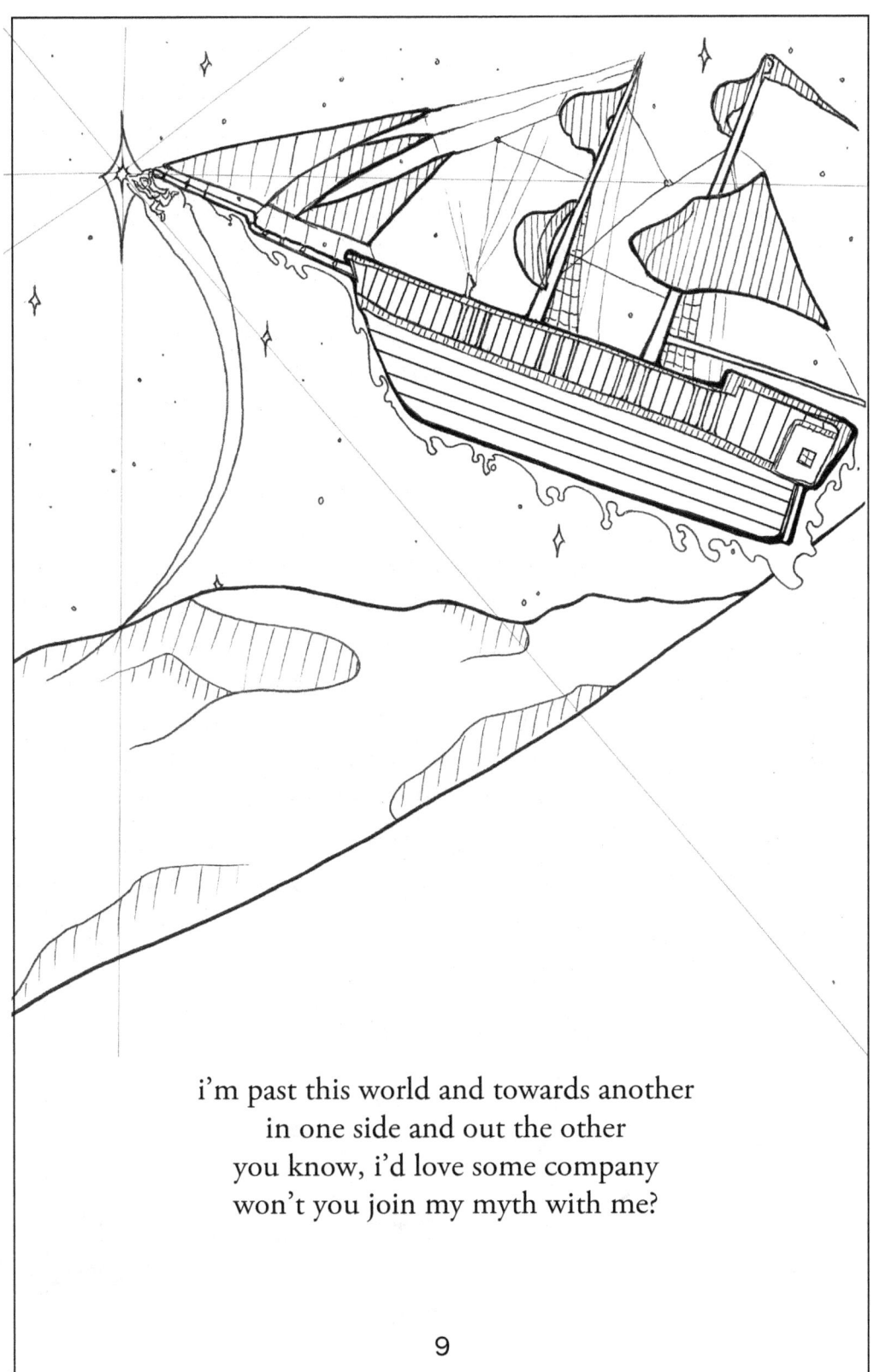

i'm past this world and towards another
in one side and out the other
you know, i'd love some company
won't you join my myth with me?

Mary's Lamb

Mary had a little lamb
on very little level land

it was silty, swarthy, salty sand
where mary had her little lamb

slowly, silently, she sat down smiling

now don't laugh or leer or say i'm lying
she minced that mutton into malleable meat
and had herself something sweet to eat

She found the taste delectable
The flavor readily detectable
sighing, she sat up from that table
ending the tale of this dark fable.

Peer Pressure

The cow jumped into the moon
didn't make it

his friends all made him do it
hoping to break it

it was then decreed
and generally agreed
that unless you're a sheep
look before you leap

Indeed

Indeed is needed less these days
but see the beauty of this phrase;

with sophistication you reply
much mystery it can supply
in anger one can express this word
and surprise describes this here adverb

Indeed.
Indeeeeed…
In-DEED!
Indeed?!?!

oh yes indeed you need to feed this seed
of fine vernacular
so do not fear my dear you'll hear right in your ear
something spectacular!

Bordumb

Hey son, what are you, bored?
there's a whole world you have ignored!

why not check out the pattern
on your walls, ceilings and floors
pretend you're on mars, neptune or saturn
pretend spacemen live in your drawers

go on and walk out your front door
or the back if the front's a chore
go lay in the grass and look at the clouds
go to the mall and just stare at those crowds

for crying out loud you're soaring through space
this world's got weird smeared all over the place
you've got one billionth of this place explored
bored? that's boring. let curiosity roar!

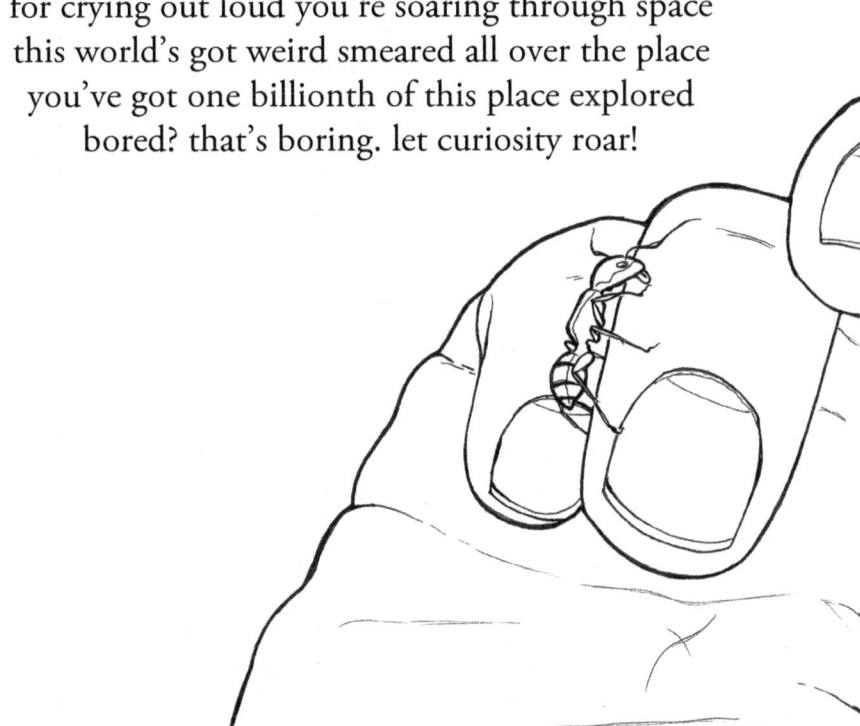

Forest Creature

Forest filters with it's trees
speckled sunlight splashes me
from the darkness comes creeping newt
exploring each wet arching root

mossy earth and humid air
fireflies over water there
hop the stream in silent shout
this is what it's all about

i'm a forest creature

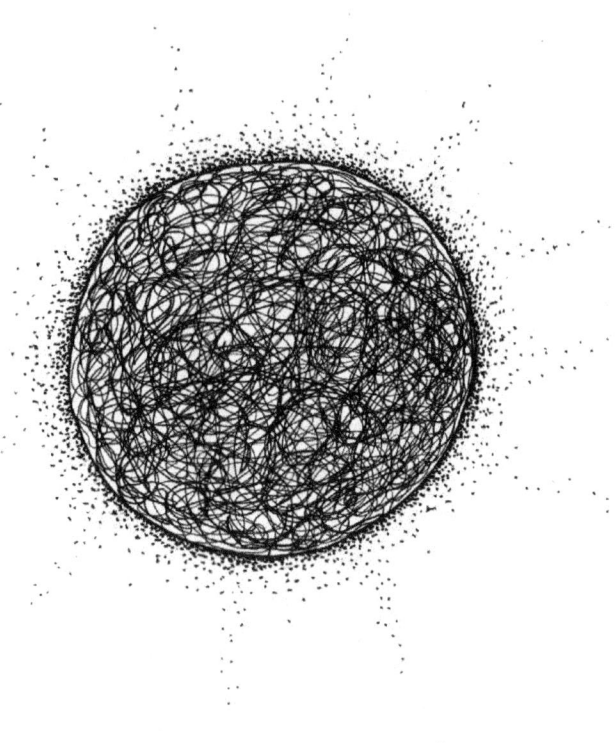

Eclipse

The sun is out
the mind is in
though i can't hear it over this din
for the thoughts of a child
are loud and wild

they are free
lost and forgotten by you and me?

The Void

As i begin to enter in
i close my eyes and look within
i take with me my vigor vim
for guts are needed to proceed
or perhaps the opposite i concede

with no up or down, left or right
i'm Guided by my hearts own light
for mind alone goes back and forth
spitting forever spiral froth

bridge the gap and let it go
dive on in until you know
what we are in truth and truth in full
we exist on every channel
we are the ever evolving mammal

Home

Drove down darkness, filtered through
the trees beset me, comfort true
moon dims stars, but cast on fields
to which playful shadows yield

walking towards this grand show
i chuckle loudly, as i know
it's all so perfect to ever miss
this ever elated inner bliss

laying down on ancient land
raising up my outstretched hand
i am by myself, but not alone
for i am also
this great unknown

Wake Walking

I woke up today
but i might still be sleeping
i'm awake i say
but the doubt comes a creeping

i fell down the stairs
but i'm gliding instead
perhaps i'm still inside my head

i wonder while i wake
where have i just been?
was that really fake?
am i back in my skin?

i fear that my dreams
may be broken
this is the third time
i have woken

well whatever, fine, i'll just go with it
how long has it been?
i start to forget

is this real? does it actually matter?
i now feel just a bit towards the latter

i've never found anything wrong
being where you truly belong
away i go, i'm leaving, i'm gone
don't wait up, i could be long

the truth is here
and miles away
we are all dreaming
in our own way

Old Man of the Sea

There goes the old man of the sea
already armored for under the ocean
down to the knobs of his knees

a breeze bellows in from the buoy of tin
that pumps air down to the deep
he skips with a grin as he steps on a fin
of a shark, in the sand, asleep

the shark shot up and sank its incisors
into the leg of the man
who wondered while watching, devising a plan
of how shark might taste in a pan

the old man of the sea, as mean as can be
reached underneath and broke all it's teeth
when he punched that fish in the chin

he dragged it's tail back and made a fine snack
of fish fingers, fries, and fillet
patting his belly while cracking his back
he then said
"perhaps i'll go for a second today"

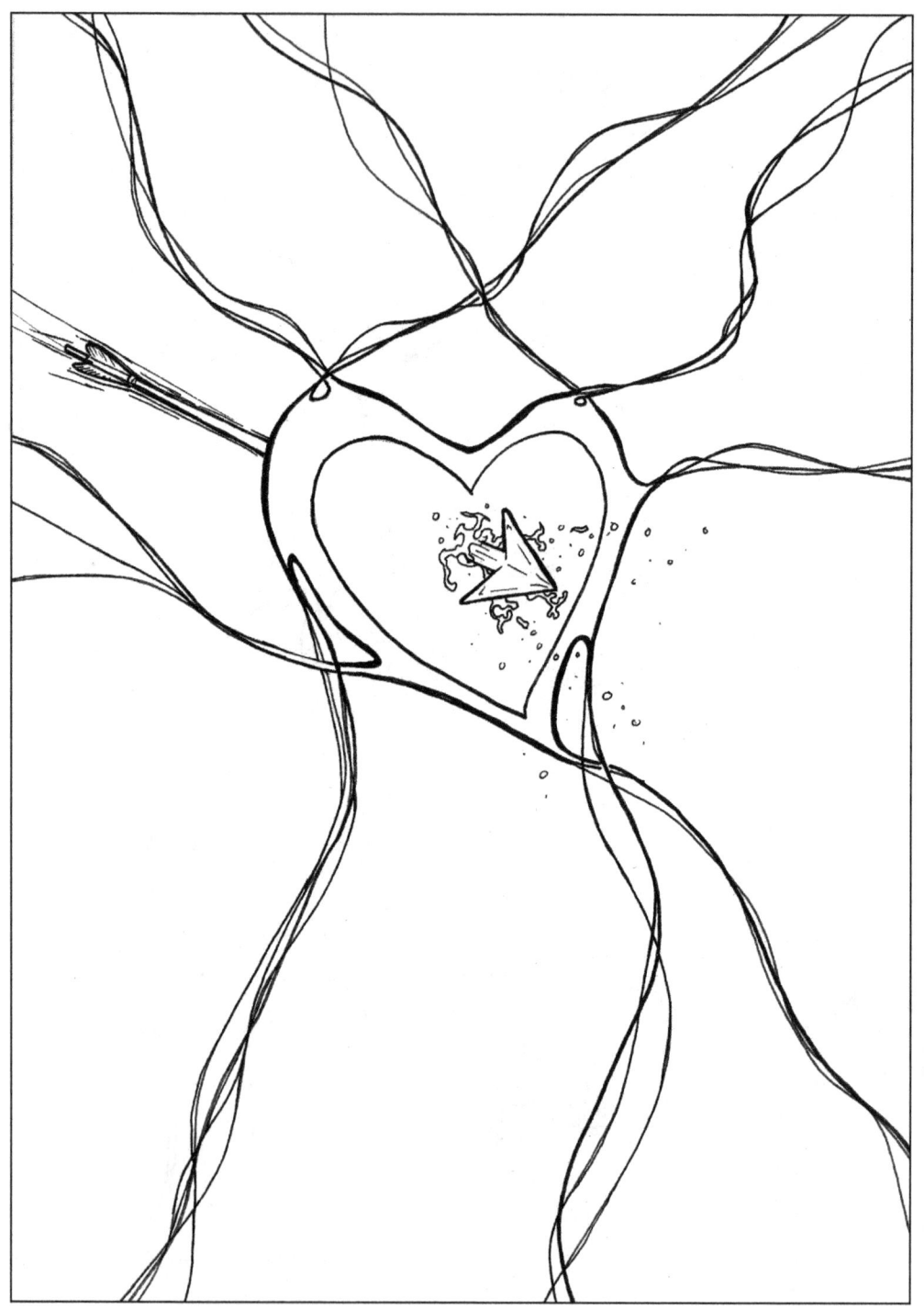

Eros

Mirth marinating in my marrow
eros aims with ethereal arrow
made of lead with a golden core
it strikes the heart that it's bound for
pulsing, pounding, pleasing feel
the arrows path begins to heal

how have i ever thought
i was separate?
this new bond we've wrought
i will temper it

we never need complete each other
we who now reflect one another
i know myself when I look upon you
you return my gaze and see it too

i will serve as your reservoir
because i love you
for who you are

Hubbard

Old mother hubbard, kept cats in her cupboard
her morbid skills she would hone
she would wait while sitting
and bake them while knitting
cooking those kitty cat scones

she used to be, you see
a cat lady
until things got a bit out of hand

she needed to feed, oh yes indeed
two hundred cats from across the land

but, oh these cats, oh so many?
what to do with them all?
easy you see, just a penny
at "Hubbard's Bakery Stall"

that old mother hubbard, she kept cats in her cupboard
yes those kitties of the countryside
the ones we've adored, oh yes oh lord
we've all been taken for a ride

Magic

The secret of magic is in this verse
within accordance to the universe
uni is one, all that can be
verse is a line of poetry

in a form of cosmic digestion
we are all answering the question
of who we really are
as does every insect, animal
planet and star

all the cells in your hand
are under your command
but who are they really?

they are the gods
whom we're god of
now isn't that odd?

and now you know
as above, so below

we are the same
its the greatest kind of game
of becoming ourselves sincerely

Mermaiden

Woe is you & me, for what a sight is she
from tail to her hip, she comes fully equipped
to whirl up a pooling of dancing frenzy

she comes from the sea and is pleased as can be
that the movement and motion she knows from the ocean
is also above in the air

she then goes about, turning tail to toe
and smiles as her legs begin to grow
her new limbs she wiggles
her new rump she jiggles
a glistening goddess i do suppose
whose very visage glimmers and glows
i'd guarantee if you saw, you'd agree
oh what a sight is she

it is her code to leave her watery abode
to find one lucky mortal, open a portal
and have upon him, her love, bestowed

and who would it be
but little old me
the lock to her key
opened and free

my friend, my friend, i say with glee
oh what a sight is she

Ridiculous

With silly things i agree
i don't take life too seriously
people's expressions scrunch in oddly
they say i'm daft and say it proudly

"not a lick of sense, that's why he's daffy!"
"no one should always be so happy!"

i smile and let them think as they do
knowing quite the opposite is true
for everyone always, always forgets
we're all actually spacemonkey cadets

we're all on a rock that's hurtling with grace
spinning round and round a fireball in space
pacing billions of others on a galactic race
into a massive black hole's loving embrace

galaxies are actual living things
notes in a song the universe sings

can you all now please agree with me
how silly it is to even be?

next time your accused of being nonsensical
tell them that their minds are infinitesimal!
i can't think of a thing more hideous
then a space ape that's serious...
that's just being ridiculous!

Lost

Oh some day you may get lost
not on a street but life itself
so make a list of things to do
but really try and think them through

it's not your stuff now or what you will have
it's the things you take with you when you die
like how many times you could laugh
or how many rules you could defy

it's adventure and the experience
it's what you change and your friend's alliance
it's the things you cannot ever hold
it's what you think back on when you're old

you move through life by what you desire
do as you will but please remember
we come from the same source, somewhere higher
we all are part of that burning ember
that sparks a flame every once in a while
throwing into the world both form and style

be that fire for every one of us
do well for others and forget the fuss
of those that have now lost their way
for those sad sunken souls that toil away
in the muck of the world, in dirt, in dust
lost in lands of material lust

go, be free, invert yourself
then you'll know what is real wealth

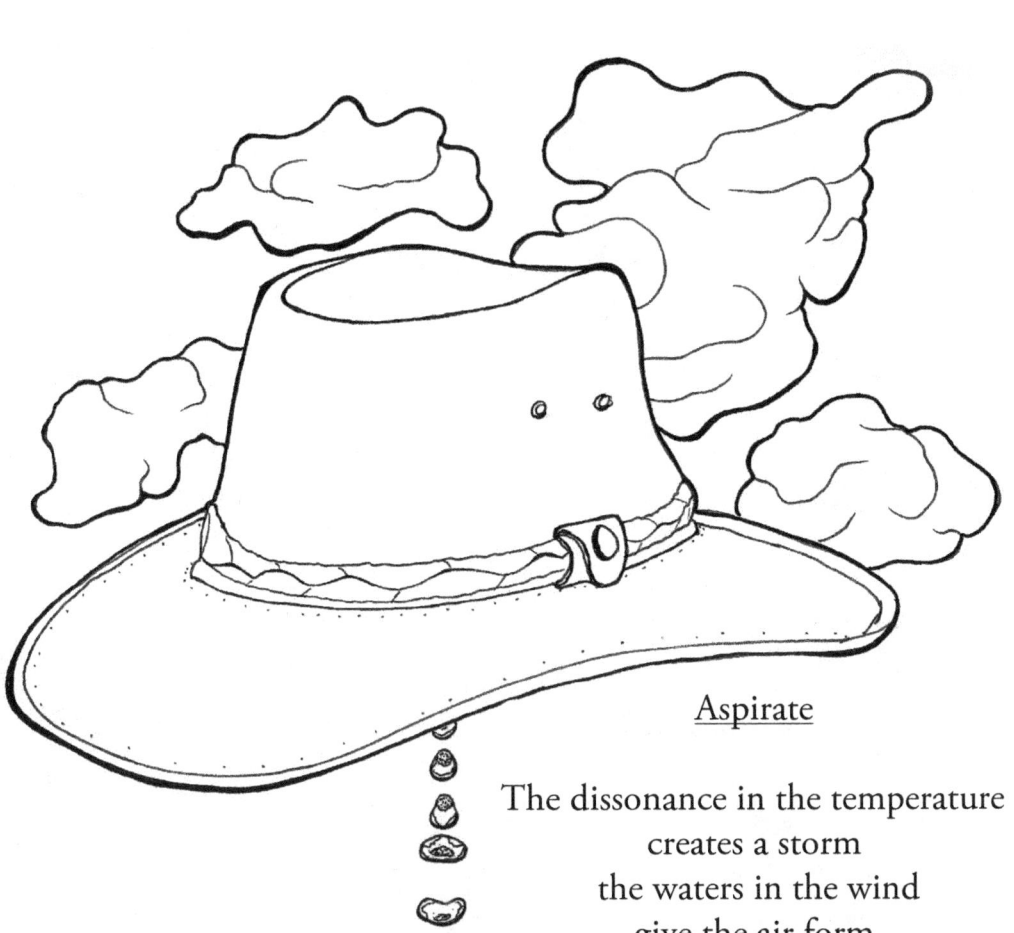

Aspirate

The dissonance in the temperature
creates a storm
the waters in the wind
give the air form
the hat on my head
keeps my thoughts warm
stirring slowly
they soon start to swarm

like rain on the pond
they create a movement
now invisible forces
become apparent

beauty is truth
shown how to behave
the source of the shadows
dancing in this cave.

The Sandman

In midst of sleep
i do creep
in and out of dream
what i seek
i do keep
are ingredients that do gleam

you see i sell solution salves
for the bodies dreaming valves
and as it drips on down the throat
you will then begin to note

the motion of my mixes fixes
emotional convictions which
permeates your person

that gentle, stirring, whirling
of enlightened unfurling
varies with every version

a touch herein will awaken within
conclusions to confusions that have patterns like plaid
solutions to delusions you did not know you had

drink it down; you'll feel a zing
where your wonder does take wing
and soon your soul will start to sing
come on in, look around, my solution salve shop
because i'm the Sandman
and
my prices can't be topped

Magnetism

By the way did you know?
that dreams & wishes are seeds you sow?

it's easy to see, less for you than me, but eventually

you'll find that whatever you want will come to you
if you believe it like you breathe, it will come true
don't want it and whine and wonder where it is
you can choose your reality; realize this!

now it will work for almost everything
so use it well and not for petty things
bring friends and adventure and a life filled with love
pack your life like a suitcase, closed with a shove

your powers of belief will open the door
now just be careful what you are wishing for!

The Star Catcher

The star catcher drifts through the dream of the night
filling it's net with falling points of light
no one knows why or for what purpose it does
but many suspect, it's just because.

flying, falling while slipping and gripping
it's endless catcher that's slightly ripping
no stars escape but the dust drifts down
to land in the dreams of the various towns.

the children who woke to next mornings light
found that the dusting had enhanced their sight
"i can see forever" one child claimed
"i can see farther then that!" another exclaimed

adults of the towns all gathered around
to try and figure out what could be done
they whispered and worried in hush tones of hurry
until a man spoke of his son.

"my boy says he can see nine hundred shades of blue,
worse then that, he's gone an named them all too!"

"my girl says she sees we all live forever,
and not to worry, there's no such thing as never"

"my kid told me that nothing is at all what it seems,
that what we think of the world is just a thick dream"

"he then said his mind had been freed, thoughts are seeds,
and my aura was a particular shade of sea foam green!"

the adults all began yelling in bellowing shouts
clamoring to express the degree of their doubts
the frightened grownups could not choose a choice
until the eldest council woman had cleared her voice

"i don't know what is with this fighting and fuss,
the problem isn't with them, it lies within us.
our children know something we've long forgot,
it's something we need and we need it a lot.
just because it's different, don't lose your reason.
remember, we must love every season"

the grownups going home stopped listening to fears
and began listening with their own ears
the children were waiting with a gleam in their eye
to show the adults the stars in the sky.

practical parents are right more often then not
but kids know a world that grownups forgot
we depend on each other, the young and the old
as we love one another it comes back tenfold

so keep your feet on the earth and your head in space
and look for that star catcher's celestial chase!

Lost Unicorn

Have you seen my unicorn?
you would know it by it's horn
it's pure white and glows with magic
losing it would be rather tragic

it ran right this way i could have sworn
are you *sure* you haven't seen my unicorn?
i've heard they are very hard to steal
mostly because no one knows they're real

perhaps it joined a unicorn migration,
or packed up a suitcase and went on vacation
i guess it's gone, i'm sure i'm at fault
i should have invested in a unicorn vault

to hold all the things i've lost, i'd need a wagon

come to think of it, seems i've misplaced my
dragon...

Ode to the Armadillidiidae

The pill bug to some, is nothing but an insect
but thinking like that is caused by a defect
lack of wonder for the world is what they missed
small truths unfurled cannot be dismissed.

start paying attention to what goes on below
we're creatures unknown to the microcosmic flow
roly poly, chiggy-wigs, potato bugs:
these little guys can give themselves hugs!

Ar·ma·dil·li·di·i·dae
sound it out, it's fun to say
armadillidiidae, if you see one let it lay
it's copper based body bleeds blue blood
minding it's business it cleans up crud
no longer do you have to guess or suppose
who's responsible for what will decompose

if your kind you'll find,
there is nothing really odd
about loving this little isopod.

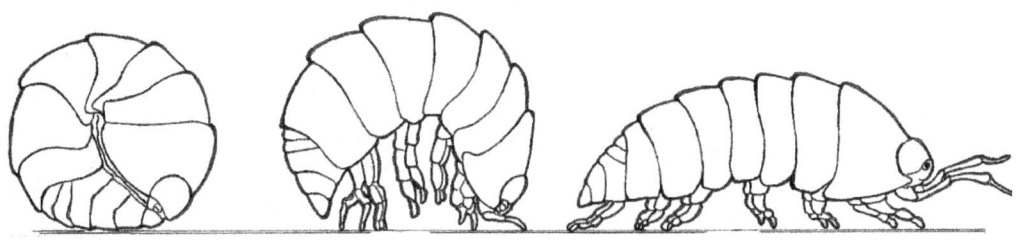

One Red Ball

One red ball does bounce and fall
through hills and valleys and the world throughout
as ball does bounce and begin to roll
it picks up the perceptions of the towns about

each person ball passes, it ponders what they know
each bounce belays the belief of folk down below
and when ball loses its momentum and stops with a grind
ball realizes separate realities resides in each person's mind
life and death and the meaning of it all
like baby's breath, come the thoughts of said ball

people in this world see what they will
whether it's love or loss or the urge to kill
it's a meeting of worlds with each passing gaze
right & wrong like black & white are just varying grays

ball enjoys its recent rest, its insides full
and muses to itself, like everything else
it is in truth, but a circle.

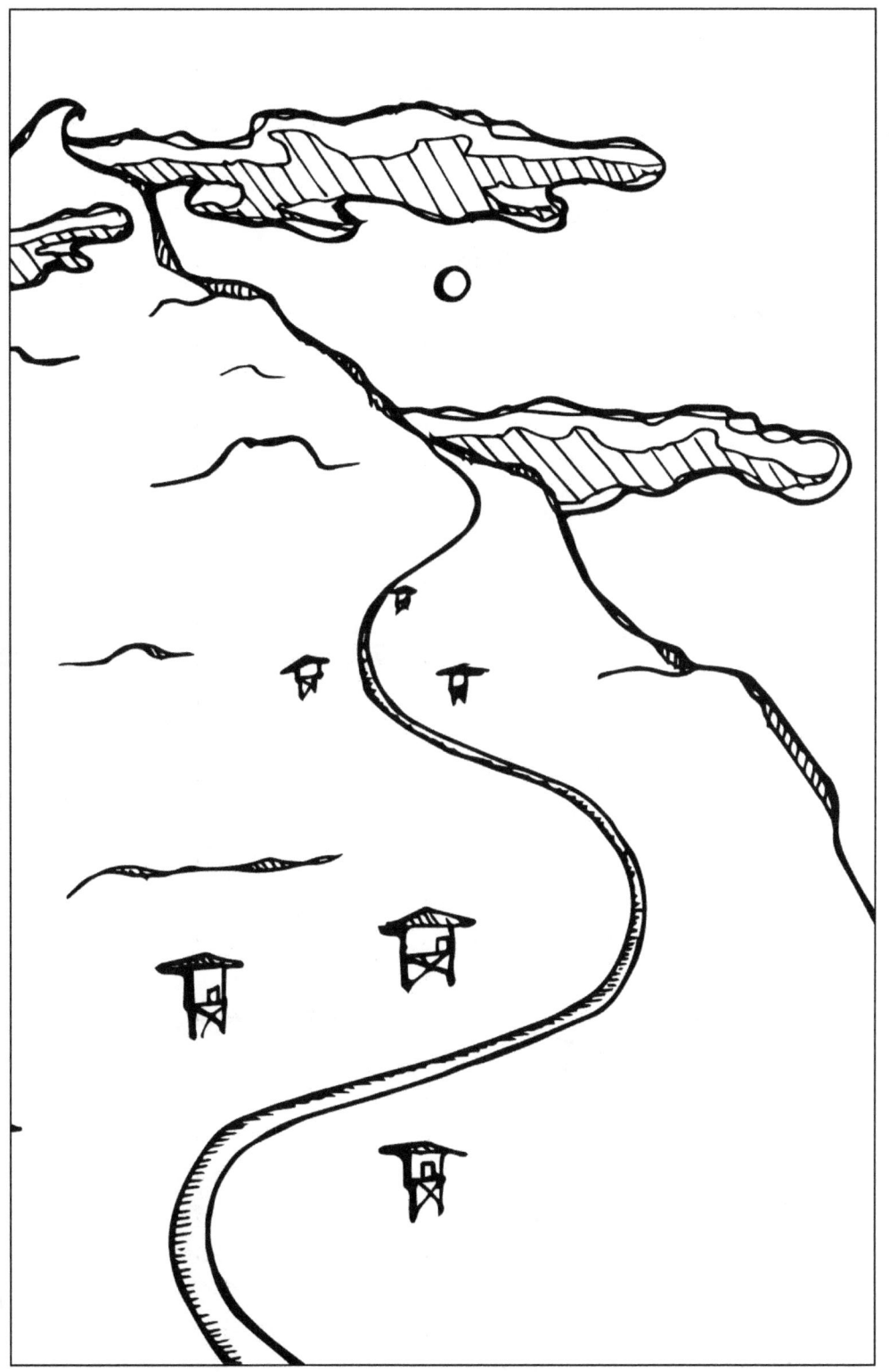

There are gods in us
as we are also in them
mine hides in my grin

I whistle to stone
but much more often to trees
never mind the tune

The Dark Knight

The dark knight burst onto hallowed ground
surrounded suddenly by oaks circled round
gossamer maidens came down from the leaves
and started to sing, dancing in the trees

the sound reached a crescendo, then gave birth
to the dark knight, who thrust blade into earth
climbing up the sword, his arm, was white
it reached his feet and exploded with light

he burst into diamonds of electric glitter
changing from darkness to lightning transmitter
the glade was vaporized, the knight shot up
breaching the heavens, he emptied his cup

joining points of brightness up in the sky
he fell with other stars, from far up high
where he hit a lone figure grew
dispersing into us; yes, me and you

he is light and hope and redemption for all
he is the force that tears down all your walls
resounding loudly from an ethereal horn:

the once dark knight is now reborn

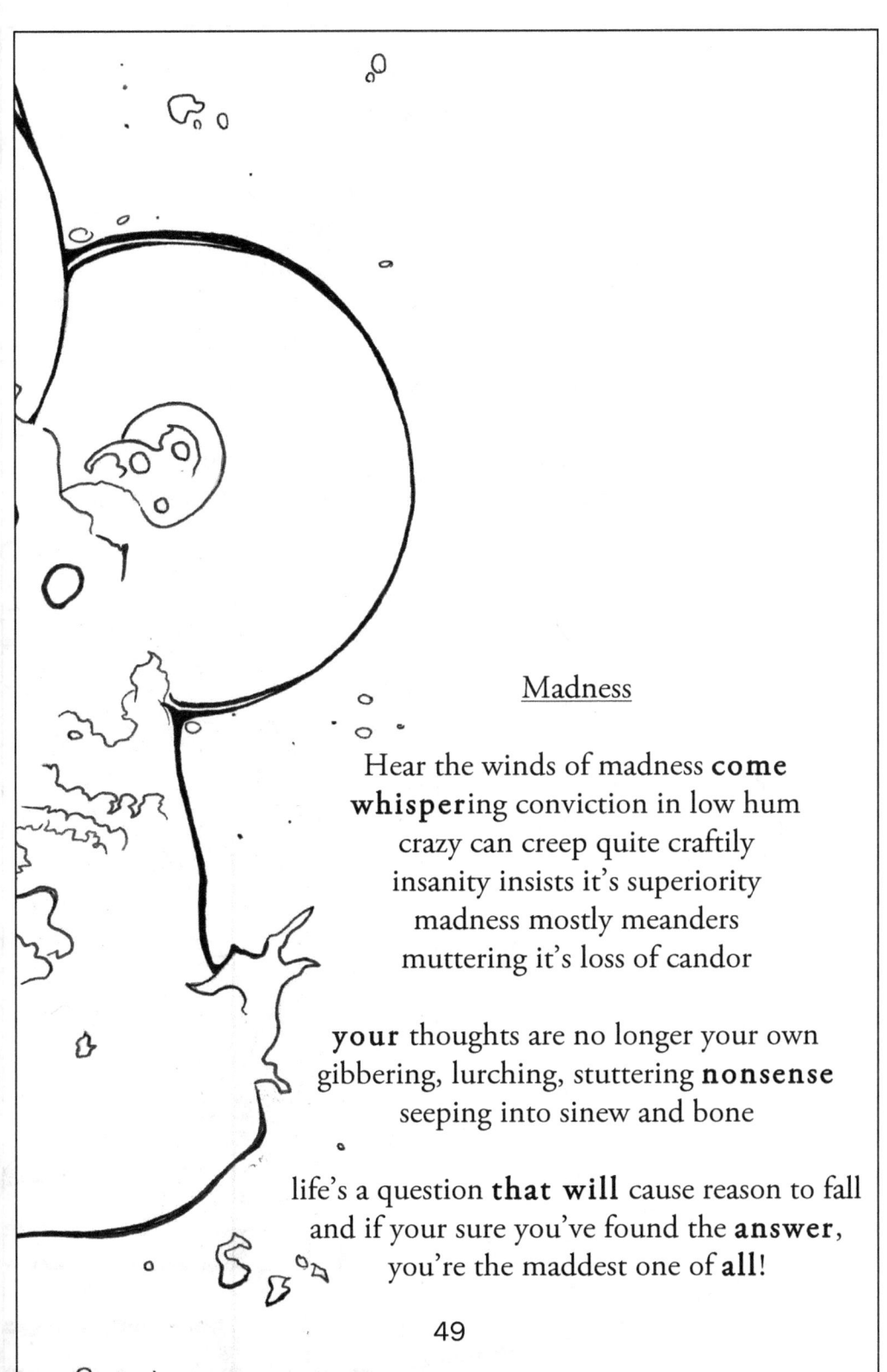

Madness

Hear the winds of madness **come
whisper**ing conviction in low hum
crazy can creep quite craftily
insanity insists it's superiority
madness mostly meanders
muttering it's loss of candor

your thoughts are no longer your own
gibbering, lurching, stuttering **nonsense**
seeping into sinew and bone

life's a question **that will** cause reason to fall
and if your sure you've found the **answer**,
you're the maddest one of **all**!

Biorhythmic

Biographic biology building better bodies
Infinite infinity looping life lovely
Void-death re-birth repeating odyssey

Presto manifesto presents poignant proof
That reality ripples beneath your roof

Fine mind vine wine leaves throat shouting serendipic lines
Space-time laced rhymes with mind mining synchronistic signs

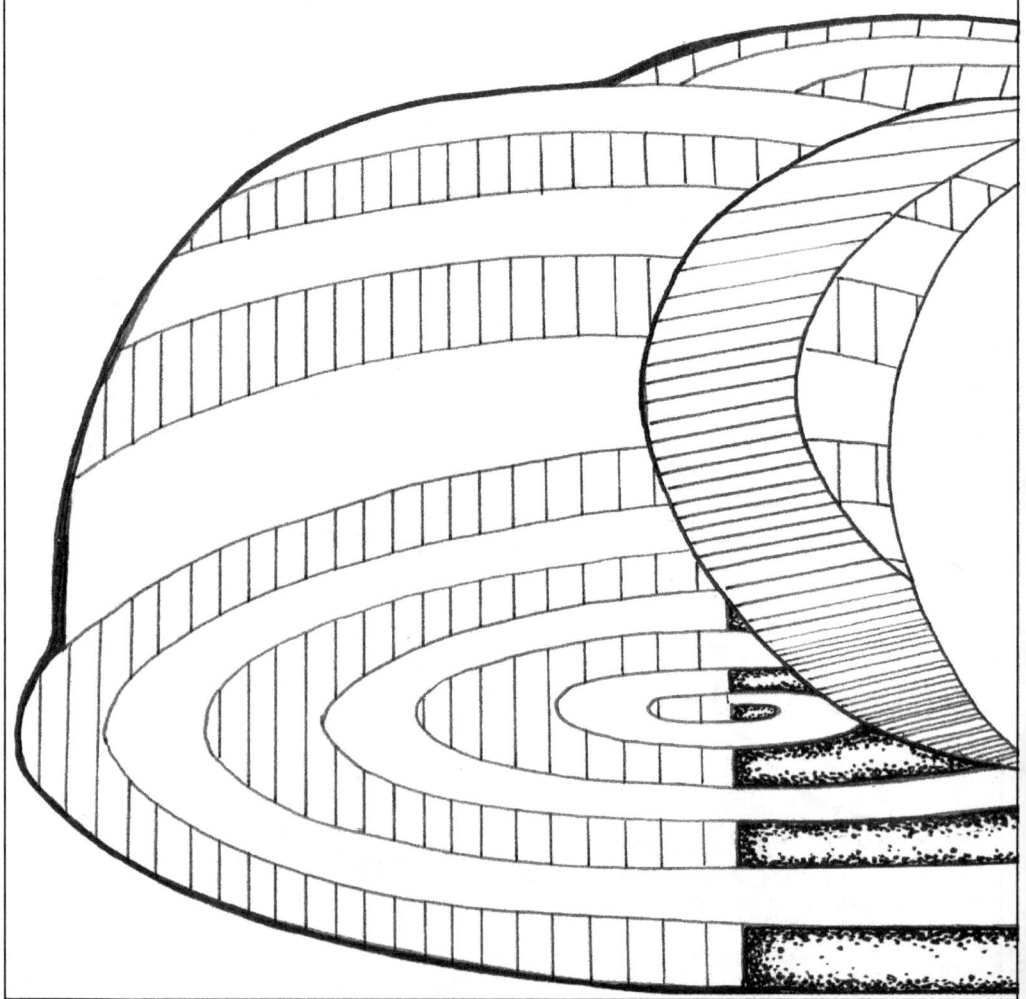

lazy leg lounging leads to comfy cozy
kind cuddling
crazy beg scrounging pleads to come free my noisy
mind muddling
those intermingling tingling limbs form
memory puddling
that spur single jingling within and swarm
my merry stuttering

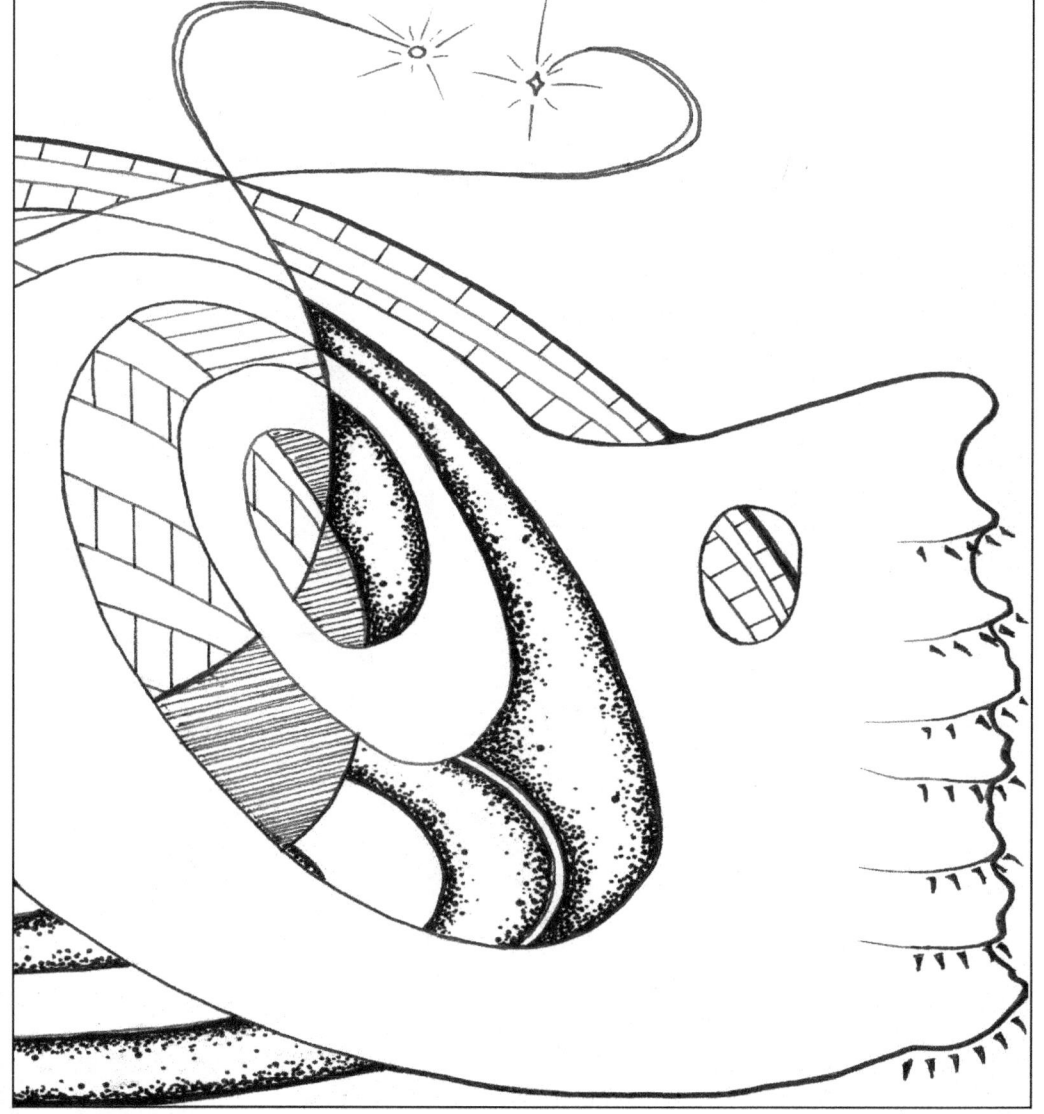

The Rhizome Remains

Flowers are fleeting
but the rhizome remains

the petals that fall
make room for the seed
unfolding the old
for the earth to feed

from rhizome to flower
to seed on the ground
each stage of the cycle
goes round and round

what seems to be dying
is just transforming
like the turning of the world
that moves night to morning

nothing is lost, it's all retained
just like the rhizome
that always remains

www.ingramcontent.com/pod-product-compliance
Lightning Source LLC
Chambersburg PA
CBHW070802050426
42452CB00012B/2459